THE
BLACK
BACK-UPS

THE BLACK BACK-UPS

POETRY BY KATE RUSHIN

Firebrand
Books
Ithaca, New York

Earlier versions of some of the work in this book have appeared in the following books and periodicals: *An Ear To The Ground: Contemporary American Poetry* (University of Georgia Press), *Black/Out, Conditions, Dark Horse, Home Girls: A Black Feminist Anthology* (Kitchen Table Press), *Real Paper, Shankpainter, Small Moon, Sojourner, This Bridge Called My Back: Writing by Radical Women of Color* (Persephone/Kitchen Table Press), and *The Women's Review of Books.*

Book design by Bets Ltd.
Cover design by Lee Tackett
Typestting by Bets Ltd.

Printed on acid-free paper in the United States by McNaughton & Gunn

Library of Congress Cataloging-in-Publication Data

Rushin, Kate, 1951–
    The Black back-ups : poetry / by Kate Rushin.
      p.   cm.
    ISBN 1–56341–026–5 (cloth) : ISBN 1–56341–025–7 (paper)
    1. Afro-American—Poetry.   I. Title.
PS3568.U7277B58   1993
811'.54—dc20   92–46886
                                               CIP

ACKNOWLEDGMENTS

Many people have supported me over the years. Special thanks and appreciation goes to the New Words Bookstore Collective, Rita Arditti, Gilda Bruckman, Madge Kaplan, Mary Lowry, Jean MacRae, Joni Seager and Laura Zimmerman. Thanks to Cynthia Enloe, Judith Wachs, Joseph Shay, Marion Lill, Marjorie Posner, Barbara Smith, Gloria Anzaldúa, Cheryl Clarke, Cherríe Moraga, Judith Steinbergh, Evelyn C. White, Martin Espâda, Jack Powers, Robin Becker, Kathy Aguero, Barbara Helfgott Hyett, Rosario Morales, Dick Levins, Thomas Grimes, Philip Robinson, Darryl Alladice, Barbara Herbert, Molly Snyder, Michelle Turre, Gary Friedman, Clover Chango, Pat Bell Scott, Shani Doud, Diane Meier, Warren Sherman, Genita Ekpenyong, Michelle Baxter, Michelle Gabow, Sharon Cox, Becky Johnson, Jaqui Alexander, Ginny Chalmers, Floyd Barbour, Marilyn Richardson, Florance Ladd, Diane Hamer, Keitha Fine, Irene Handshuch, Paula Ebron, E. Fran White, Andrea Benton Rushing, Becky Thompson, Mary Gilfus, Jeanne Hubbuch, Nancy Hughes, Mary Mason, Ruth Perry, Sandy Martin, Tatiana Schreiber, Stephanie Poggie, Eileen Bolinsky, Melanie Berzon, Shelley V. Smith, Lisa Hirsch, Rod Kessler, Maxine Feldman, Deborah Silverstein, Ellen K. Wade, Maureen Brodoff, Suze Prudent, Calvin Hernton, Susan Eshbach, Beverly Smith, Margaret Warren, Steve Seidel, Nancy, Dickie, and Adria, Angela Bowen, Jennifer Abod, Angela Gillem, Paul Guilfoyle, Anita Jamieson, Monique Monroe, Ginny Berkowitz.

Thanks to the Artists' Foundation, Cummington Community of the Arts, Fine Arts Work Center in Provincetown, Ellen LaForge Memorial Foundation/Grolier Bookshop, Ann Stokes Lecture Series, Alice Belton Lecture Series, Rachel Guido deVries and the 1991 Feminist Women's Writing Workshop, and Jean Caiani of Speak Out!

Special thanks and love to Frank D. Rushin, Charlotte Spear, and the Rushin/Wiggins Family; Helen B. Morales, Eleanor Williams, Constance Williams Wilson, Hilda Hicks, Breda V. Williams, Ernestine Thomas, Isaac Williams, Leon Williams, John Peter Williams, and the Williams/Arthur Family; the Glovers and the Bournes. For being there down that crucial last-mile-of-the-way, I'd like to thank Audre Lorde, Patricia Powell, Jewelle Gomez, Evelynn Hammonds, Sakia Yasmine, Mimi Brown, Nina de Maia, Janeen Green, Carleasa Coates, Mary McDonagh and the staff of the Brown University Computing Resource Center, and Nancy K. Bereano of Firebrand Books.

For My Family

In Memory of My Grandparents
Addie O. Arthur Williams (1896-1964)
George E. Williams, Sr. (1891-1975)
Roxie Wiggins Rushin Edwards (189?-1984)

and My Mother
B. Elizabeth Williams Rushin (1922-1962)

and for Audre Lorde (1934-1992)

CONTENTS

When I came home, the weeping willow had finally fallen. There used to be snapdragon, cockscomb and chrysanthemum. There was an apple tree, a dogwood, a mimosa. And there were roses! Twenty tons of roses! I haven't seen Floating Island Pudding since Sunday Dinner: white linen tablecloth, yellow cake no icing, lemons snuck out of the ice-tea glasses. Nobody at the school had ever heard of it. Maybe Gramom made it up. The island part is beaten egg whites. The pudding is the water.

FAMILY TREE

for Addie O. Williams

I come from
A long line of
Uppity Irate Black Women
Although they were
Church people
And I'm the only one
Who drinks and cusses
Let me tell you
When those ladies got going
They had no match
You think I'm bold
Imagine my Grandmother Addie
Raising her umpteen children
During the Depression
Imagine the audacity of
This woman who only
Went to the third grade
Joining the Book-Of-The-Month Club
She gave me a six-volume set of
The World's Best Poetry
When I was seven years old
When I was nine
My grandmother sent
A coupon and one dollar to
Nabisco Shredded Wheat
They sent her a knife
And fork and spoon
She kept them in a yellow
Envelope in the dish closet drawer
She would say they were for me
For when I went away to college

I didn't know what it meant exactly
But I would open the drawer
And look at them
And it made me feel
Real Good
And you ask me how come
I think I'm so cute
Nowadays
I cultivate
Being Uppity
It's something
My Gramom taught me
It's about time
I learned
My lesson

Gramom and my Great-Aunt Rachel sit at the kitchen table drinking Lipton tea and eating Ritz crackers with Welch's grape jelly. They talk about Cousin Henry Who Was in the Navy and Got Sent to Levenworth Down Where The Devil Shot the Owl and What Makes Bosoms Full. My Great-Aunt Rachel says that Haines ain't nothing but an old spasm anyhow. I sit with my chin propped on the table trying not to breathe. I don't want them to notice that it's late and I'm still up.

Poppy sits in his armchair in the corner with his bad leg on the piano bench. He is there first thing in the morning and last thing at night. When I hack out chords from the Methodist hymnal, he lays his head back and hums. He beats out the time with the flat of his hand.

Whenever there's a thunderstorm, my aunt puts on her sneakers. My grandmother makes us kids shut off the lights and television. We run from room to room shutting windows. We hear the dull slap of venetian blinds on the sills. Our nostrils twitch from the cool spiciness that stirs the trees and shows the silver-green undersides of the maple leaves. We must sit in chairs. We are not allowed to talk. We fidget in the grey-blue storm light, waiting. We can smell the rain coming. Lightning cracks the stillness. We hear the first thick plops of rain on dust, before the downpour comes.

Everybody says Miss Lindy Brown is a witch. On the 4th of July, she steps out with the Junior Marchers, Boy Scouts, and fire trucks. She wears scarves, bracelets, long swirling skirts and carries a ruffled white parasol. She prances. She curtsies. She throws kisses to us as we line the dusty streets. Everybody says Miss Lindy Brown is a witch. I don't doubt it for a minute. And always, she says to me, *Remember, Darling, Aunt Linda loves you.*

THE BLACK BACK-UPS

This is dedicated to Merry Clayton, Fontella Bass, Vonetta
Washington, Carolyn Franklin, Yolanda McCullough,
Carolyn Willis, Gwen Guthrie, Helaine Harris, and Darlene
Love. This is for all of the Black women who sang back-up for
Elvis Presley, John Denver, James Taylor, Lou Reed.
Etc. Etc. Etc.

I said Hey Babe
Take a Walk on the Wild Side
I said Hey Babe
Take a Walk on the Wild Side

And the colored girls say
Do dodo do do dodododo
Do dodo do do dodododo
Do dodo do do dodododo ooooo

This is for my Great-Grandmother Esther, my Grandmother
Addie, my grandmother called Sister, my Great-Aunt
Rachel, my Aunt Hilda, my Aunt Tine, my Aunt Breda,
my Aunt Gladys, my Aunt Helen, my Aunt Ellie,
my Cousin Barbara, my Cousin Dottie and my Great-Great-
Aunt Vene.

This is dedicated to all of the Black women riding on buses
and subways back and forth to the Main Line, Haddonfield,
Cherry Hill and Chevy Chase. This is for the women who
spend their summers in Rockport, Newport, Cape Cod and
Camden, Maine. This is for the women who open those
bundles of dirty laundry sent home from those ivy-covered
campuses.

My Great-Aunt Rachel worked for the Carters
Ever since I can remember
There was *The Boy*
Whose name I never knew
And there was *The Girl*
Whose name was Jane

Great-Aunt Rachel brought Jane's dresses for me to wear
Perfectly Good Clothes
And I should've been glad to get them
Perfectly Good Clothes
No matter they didn't fit quite right
Perfectly Good Clothes
Brought home in a brown paper bag
With an air of accomplishment and excitement
Perfectly Good Clothes
Which I hated

At school
In Ohio
I swear to Gawd
There was always somebody
Telling me that the only person
In their whole house
Who listened and understood them
Despite the money and the lessons
Was the housekeeper
And I knew it was true
But what was I supposed to say

I know it's true
I watch her getting off the train
Moving slowly toward the Country Squire
With their uniform in their shopping bag

And the closer she gets to the car
The more the two little kids jump and laugh
And even the dog is about to
Turn inside out
Because they just can't wait until she gets there
Edna Edna   Wonderful Edna

But Aunt Edna to me, or Gram, or Miz Johnson, or
Sister Johnson on Sundays

And the colored girls say
Do dodo do do dodododo
Do dodo do do dodododo
Do dodo do do dodododo ooooo

This is for Hattie McDaniels, Butterfly McQueen
Ethel Waters
Sapphire
Saphronia
Ruby Begonia
Aunt Jemima
Aunt Jemima on the Pancake Box
Aunt Jemima on the Pancake Box?
AuntJemimaonthepancakebox?
Ainchamamaonthepancakebox?
Ain't chure Mama on the pancake box?

Mama Mama
Get off that box
And come home to me

And my Mama leaps off that box
She swoops down in her nurse's cape
Which she wears on Sunday
And for Wednesday night prayer meeting
And she wipes my forehead
And she fans my face
And she makes me a cup of tea
And it don't do a thing for my real pain
Except she is my mama

Mama Mommy Mammy
Mam-mee Mam-mee
I'd Walk a Mill-yon Miles
For one of your smiles

This is for the Black Back-Ups
This is for my mama and your mama
My grandma and your grandma
This is for the thousand thousand Black Back-Ups

And the colored girls say
Do   dodo   do do   dodododo
do   dodo
*   dodo*
*   do*
*   do*

THE ANCESTORS

I went all the way to Africa
Searching for the mythic past
I found it on a homemade altar
Watching from a fading photograph

COMPARATIVE HISTORY: OUR STORIES

When I look into your face
I swear I see Russia and Rumania
I see thousands of faces looking out from your eyes
I see a peasant woman
Her legs strong from the fields
Drinking tea by the stove
I see a man leaning over his heavy book
I see a young girl laughing from deep in her belly
I see them
I see Molly, Rachel, Goldie and Flora
I see Harry, Albert, Carl and Ben

And when I look at you
I feel my own people gazing out from my eyes

Look and you will see a bondswoman
Her legs strong from the fields
Drinking tea by the hearth
Look and see a man rocking over his heavy book
See a young girl laughing from way deep in her belly
Look and you can see the Ashanti, the Bambara, the Fulani
You can see Mamie, Ama, Akiba and Snow Pearl
You can see Walter, Kojo, Moses and Ned

Thousands of people stretch out behind us
Like the cars of a freight

How do we compare

The Final Solution, The Peculiar Institution
The Slave Ship, The Death Train
The Gas Chamber, The Lynching Tree
The Amistad Revolt, The Warsaw Uprising
The Burned Book, The Smashed Drum
Bergen-Belsen and Cape Coast Castle

Do we dare compare our terrible histories

It would have been easy for neither of us to be here
If someone had stayed a day too long. . .
If someone had left a day too soon. . .

But here we are
Meeting by chance
As people do
The daughter of Marilyn and Birdie, Sol and Jack
The daughter of Roxie and Addie, George and Issac

Here we are
To witness the dead
And the living
In each other's eyes

MAKING WAY FOR SISTER

for Roxie Wiggins Rushin Edwards

For thirty miles
The string of cars
In my grandmother's funeral procession
Laces painfully through
The red-lighted intersections

It's some kind of a miracle
No trucks ram the hearse
No sirens scream
No one cuts us off

Even in the neighborhoods
Like the ones she worked days
For decades
With no insurance

They pause
They take note
They wonder

They all make way
For the gal from Schley County, Georgia
Finally they make way for her to pass

She saved the money
Though it wasn't enough
She chose the undertaker and the plot
Close to her girl Ruth

She could go
She said
Three days without eating
And she did

What could we do
But step aside
We step aside
We make way for her to pass

THE BREAST MILK POEM

for B. Elizabeth Williams Rushin

What makes bosoms full
Is it beer or hot tea
A man makes your bosoms full
Don't let anyone touch them

No one knows it
But I have a
Jar of mother's milk
My very own mother's milk
She puts it in the freezer
Like five loaves of bread on sale
I sit with my jar in the dark
Under the dining room table
I taste a little taste
Make it last

My mother always sits in the chair
Back against the stove
I sit straddled on her lap
With my long legs dangling
Let me tell you a secret I say
I love you these many times
I count between each quick kiss
Stop all of a sudden   Oh
My teeth hurt her lip

At night she says this:
In the winter we put
Cucumbers and vinegar in jars
And bury them by the big pine tree
We dig up pickles in the spring

She sings about peace and the valley
While she irons in the cellar
Let me lay in the bed while you make it
Takes me for walks in the park
Tell me about stone soup
Shows me Orion and The Dipper
Please sing "Danny Boy"

All the kids come running down
Back up and across the street
They hope she is teaching their class today
I walk along the curb
I let them crowd around and
Hold her hand
She is in my room
The principal has me hang up her coat
At the end of the day
I wait while she signs out
Then we walk home together
In school I never call her Mommy

Wednesdays are my favorite
On Wednesdays I sleep with
My mother while my father
Goes to the barber and to the
Bar to drink more beer
When he comes home
He carries me back to my bed
Or sometimes
I get to sleep in the middle

I climb out of my
Window and get stuck
On the back porch roof
Mommy comes and
Helps me back in
She hugs me and cries
She makes me promise
Not to do it again

I buy blue Christmas
Earrings from the 5&10
They look so nice with
Her blue hat and blue
Two-piece Sunday suit

Maybe I'm supposed to cry but
I just stand there
I don't tell her I love her or
Press my face into the
Soapy smelling pleats, the
Warm bulge of her stomach
She doesn't say
Don't worry don't cry
Does not pull me to her

I don't run down the steps
Shouting wait
I look out the window
The screen is patched
She is shaking her head
No   not the stretcher

The sun and trees and wind
Make moving shadows
On the wall
I don't know what that
Not talking
Not touching
Not moving
I don't know
What that look means

Wide feet
Swollen at the ankles
Pink on the bottoms
Dark chocolate on top
Always make me cry

Reba is a State Child and what you call fast. She wears short, tight, straight skirts and smokes cigarettes on the corner under the firehouse tree. She styles her hair in a French Roll. She comes to my house to teach me how to do the Boogaloo, the African Twist and the Philly Dog (banned in three states). My grandfather says: *Reba is too grown for you. I don't think she should come here anymore.* The next thing I hear, Reba is pregnant and tries to kill herself. I never ask anyone to my house again.

HOME

Is the split in my tongue
In my head
Where decisions are knives
In my gut

I know King Solomon's baby
She splits from the inside   out

THE BRIDGE POEM

I've had enough
I'm sick of seeing and touching
Both sides of things
Sick of being the damn bridge for everybody

Nobody can talk to anybody without me   Right

I explain my mother to my father my father to my little sister my
little sister to my brother my brother to the White Feminists the
White Feminists to the Black Church Folks the Black Church Folks
to the ex-Hippies the ex-Hippies to the Black Separatists the Black
Separatists to the Artists and the Artists to the parents of my
friends...

Then
I've got to explain myself
To everybody

I do more translating than the U.N.

Forget it
I'm sick of filling in your gaps
Sick of being your insurance against
The isolation of your self-imposed limitations
Sick of being the crazy at your Holiday Dinners
The odd one at your Sunday Brunches
I am sick of being the sole Black friend to
Thirty-four Individual White Folks

Find another connection to the rest of the world
Something else to make you legitimate
Some other way to be political and hip
I will not be the bridge to your womanhood
Your manhood
Your human-ness

I'm sick of reminding you not to
Close off too tight for too long

Sick of mediating with your worst self
On behalf of your better selves

Sick
Of having
To remind you
To breathe
Before you
Suffocate
Your own
Fool self

Forget it
Stretch or drown
Evolve or die

You see   it's like this
The bridge I must be
Is the bridge to my own power
I must translate
My own fears
Mediate
My own weaknesses

I must be the bridge to nowhere
But my own true self
It's only then
I can be
Useful

Miss Mary 'n' Martha run the little candy store down by the caterpillar tree. We run on tiptoe past the bits of fuzz mashed into the pavement. We buy red licorice, Mary Janes, and Squirrel Nut Zippers that stick to our teeth and make them ache. Miss Mary 'n' Martha wear long aprons and never smile. We don't know which one is which.

Penny has freckles and red hair and a process. Man, can that Penny skate. On Colored Night, down Watsontown, he rolls onto the rink with his shirt tied up so his belly shows. To tease each other the boys snicker and say, *Hey Man, I saw you and Penny in the milkweeds last night.* He swoops. He glides. Penny has red hair and skin the color of sand.

THE INVISIBLE WOMAN

It is sometimes advantageous to be unseen,
although it is most often rather wearing on the nerves.

Ralph Ellison/*Invisible Man*

I am The Invisible Woman
Super Woman
Wonder Woman
Afro Woman
The Woman with Triple Vision
I listen to men talk about
Schemes for picking up young girls
And broads who only rate C-minus
I listen to white people in white rooms
Sipping white wine
Talking about how this Hungarian poet
Sounds just like a
Mississippi Delta Blues singer
I listen to my relatives talk about
Homos, fags, fairies
And that girl who walks like a man
Something tells me
I was not supposed to hear this
Something tells me
I was not supposed to see this
Something tells me
I was not supposed to be here
Something tells me
You do not see me

I am Invisible Woman
The itch in the middle of your back
The mosquito in your ear
The bone in your throat
The meat
Between
Your teeth

WHEN AN OLD MAN DIES

for George E. Williams, Sr.

When an old man dies
A young man dies
A smooth man stewing chicken and
Dumplings, butchering hogs
A steady man selling fish
Riding a motorbike
Asking the blessing
Spitting on the top of a cake
He made himself

It's no surprise
But when an old man dies
A laughing, roaring
Bull-headed boy dies too
A tall boy in faded knickers
Dusty high-topped shoes
A girl's first beau
A boy's good buddy
Somebody's daddy

There's a little boy
There's a little girl
Poppy   Poppy

When my gramom got baptized at Grace Temple, she unbraided her long grey hair and wore a white gown. She stepped down into the fount. The preacher dipped her three times.

ROSA REVISITED

for Mrs. Rosa Parks, activist

Quietly rough
Tough quiet
A dignified riot
Quietly outrageous
Rough righteous
Up/right/us
Up/lift/us
Connect us
Quietly bless us
Rough righteous
Right time
Right now time
Think how time
Do it now time
Decidedly quiet
Correct us
Caress us
Connect us
Encourage us
In/courage/us
In/rage/us
We walked/we walked/we walked
It was our hurts
Our lives
Our minds
Our time

Who said
Who was it said
When was it ever
It was never
About
Anybody's
Aching feet

We play in the Do-It-Yourself family rooms, attics and garages that never get done. That pink stuff is just like cotton candy. Except it itches. On muggy days when the wind is right, our eyes burn and water. Our bare arms and legs itch. Everywhere you look is pink and hazy from the factory just outside town. That stuff is just like cotton candy. Except it itches.

HAVE YOU SEEN THEM?

Little kids who don't take
No kinda stuff offa nobody
Cuss out police cars
Bop at six
Rap at seven
Have you seen that mean
Four-foot high one-arm lean
If you don't watch out
They'll look you dead in the face
Cuss you out too

(Mess with them?
Me?
Not me
Me and my Afro
African prints
Swahili
Pierced nose
Nigerian summers
Five earrings in each ear
Twenty silver West Indian bracelets and
Thirty shelves of Black Studies paperbacks
UHURU!
Not me!
Me
Mature and Realistic
Thinking of my Future
And my car note
Maintaining my lifestyle
I know how to act
I'm a Young Bright Black Professional

In other words
A nice colored girl
Is this what they mean
By planned obsolescence?)

But have you seen them in the museum
With their faces pressed to the glass
Did you hear them ask you to lift them up
Cause they couldn't see
Have you seen them
Look at you with their mouths hanging open
Trying to see if you do what you say you do
Have you seen them frown and not know what to say
When you tell them they can have
Hotdogs or hamburgers or both if they want
Have you seen how they lean forward in their seats
Cause the Culture-In-The-Schools-Abstract-Dance-Company
Is at least Something Happening
Have you seen the way they look at you
When you tell them they have a birthday too

Little kids who don't take
No kinda stuff off nobody
Cuss out police cars
Bop at six
Rap at seven
If you don't watch out
Look you dead in the face
Cuss you out too
Little kids who don't take
No kinda stuff
Offa nobody

Our second-grade teacher, Mrs. Ionelli, lived up the block. She had a little boy who was not allowed to play with us. We felt sorry for him standing alone in his backyard all dressed up in his white shirt, blue shorts, kneesocks, and hard, lace-up shoes, looking at us. We would take a break from our ripping and running and hopping the round-top iron fences and low hedges between the tiny yards to say Hi. We knew there was something wrong with our own teacher not letting her kid near us, but we didn't have sense enough to be mad at the time.

ONE DAY AT THE MUSEUM
OF NATURAL HISTORY

Below the inscription:

TRUTH   KNOWLEDGE   FREEDOM
A Memorial from the City of New York to
Theodore Roosevelt
President
1901-1909

Our brown and common ancestor is caught mid-stride
On a huge yellow banner hanging above the entrance
Below the banner
A bronze Teddy Roosevelt
Forges onto Central Park West
Astride his high-stepping steed
Attended by a feather-wearing Red Man and a
Shield-carrying Black Man

The horse steps above the heads of young Black men
Middle-aged Black women and
One young white woman handing out leaflets
Exposing the State Department and the Museum
In cahoots with South Africa

Someone inside calls the police who come
Hitching up their pants and fingering their billy clubs
Determined to move the protesters across the street
Where there is no one
To be made uncomfortable

The serious Brother wearing the ankh pendant
Explains to the good captain
How he himself is being used and how
If they were Hare Krishnas
No one would care enough to bother

All of this is witnessed by the young Black woman officer
Who sits in the patrol car in front of the statue and
Stares into the sideview mirror
She does not notice the Indian and the African
Carrying rifles in the folds of their robes
The short Black woman wearing a scarf and
Dingy raincoat says to anyone who wants to listen
They want to keep us dancing and I'm not going to dance

The TV will not come on until you put a quarter in the slot and push down the plunger. After a half hour the set cuts off. We ask for another. Our grandmother keeps the quarters in a mayonnaise jar on the bookcase. Every week the Motorola Man comes to empty the money box. This is the way we watch TV. This is the way we pay off the Motorola.

Wednesday night at Mt. Calvary Evening Youth Service, Sissy Wells sings, "I Had A Talk With God Last Night." It has the same tune as "I Had A Talk With My Man." She starts to cry and she can't stop. The eighteen-year-old evangelist gives the altar call and Sissy goes up to pray. Miss Jeanie, her grandmother, goes up to hold and kiss her, and she starts crying too. All the rest of us in the Junior Choir sit with her singing "King Jesus Will Roll All Burdens Away" after all the other groups go home. Everybody knows she had a baby by Emanuel Jenkins. Then he went up'side her head and joined the Navy.

A NORTHERN OHIO LOVE POEM

We spent that winter talking about spring
About how good it would feel
To kick off boots and fly kites

It didn't happen
We never did get over that heavy wool and grey
That ridiculous irritation being mad at the wind

You must've been suffocating
Your long legs jammed into those winter rooms
Full of my friends

You never said   I never asked
Now this winter I hear you've gotten crazy and pitiful
This winter they're saying the same thing about me

It's the Saturday morning before school starts and I have to have decent shoes. The place is jammed full of mirrors and cute little white kids who wear 3's and 5's. We are the only colored people here. My aunt says we want saddle oxfords. I hate saddle oxfords. Make your feet look like gunboats, submarines. The salesman has me put my foot on the odd-shaped metal foot measurer. God, how old are you? Eleven?! I sweat and my ears get hot. Hey Jerry! This kid wears a 9½! The whole place looks at me. Now I must try them out. The slick-soled shoes slide on the thick carpet. My aunt tells me to stand up straight. I can't get my legs or arms to move right. I whine. I don't want them. They don't fit right. Then I hold my breath. O.K. They're O.K. Let's go.

WHY I LIKE TO GO PLACES:
FLAGSTAFF, ARIZONA, JUNE 1978

I was not supposed to Go Places
I was not supposed to go Off The Block
To The Park
To Bad Parts of town
Or to places I'd never been before
I was not supposed to hitchhike
Or go into bars like Langston Hughes did
Or talk to men like Simple
Why can't I go   Why can't I go
Of course I knew why
Everybody knows why
But still I had to go
And that is why I bought a
$69 Anywhere-We-Go bus ticket
And that is how I came to meet George Baker
Formerly of Mobile, Alabama
Proprietor of the Rio Grande Motel
Coach of the Front End Alignments
Women's softball team and his daughter Janie
And his son-in-law Danny
And his little gran' Puddin
This is how George came to tell me in a
Slightly perplexed voice
How his ninteen-year-old daughter and her husband
Were poisoned by a gas leak in a borrowed apartment
On Christmas and weren't found until two days later
This is how I came to fix fried chicken and biscuits for George
A forty-two-year-old Black construction worker in Flagstaff
With a family of six there and a family of seven in Mobile
I also cooked for Ira

The wizened alcoholic white man who lives with him and
Watches the place during the day and worships the ground
He walks on

This how I came to read the letter that Ira's
Diabetic adopted granddaughter had written him
From the reformatory
And how I told Ira
Sure she'll come back
As the tears rolled down his cheeks

And this is how I came to sit in the car at the game
With George and his friend Bobby drinking beer
While Bobby told how Ellie's boy
The one who had got put out on the street
Was found dead in an abandoned house and nobody knew why
Except it might've been drugs or pneumonia or a combination
And George shook his head and sighed and
Figured it didn't do any good to talk about it

This is how I came to be riding around in the car with George
And up to the top of the hill overlooking the city
And past the University where his wife works as a secretary
And this is how I came to be sitting in the Homeward Bound Bar
Listening to George talk about her
His kids and his girlfriend
And his buddy Gerald
Who got shot in the back of the head by a white cop
Who said Gerald was coming at him with a gun
And how that cop knows that George knows
Who killed his buddy
And how George himself did time
And he didn't want to do it
But the boy wouldn't back off
And that's how he ended up leaving Mobile

And this is how George came to say
Shall I call you in the morning
Or shall I just lean over and whisper
I said
Call me George
And then in the morning George said
I think I'm sick
I don't think I need to go to work today

I said George
You look fine
And then we had breakfast
And then I was off to the Canyon
And then to L.A.

And all of that is why I carry a picture of a
Gold-toothed Black man from Flagstaff, Arizona
Wearing a suit and tie and stingy-brim hat

That is why I carry a picture of George in my wallet

SYRACUSE, BY NIGHT, IN TRANSIT

There must be
Something Special
Here for me

I stand outside the grey-aired bus station
Beneath the overpass
Looking up and down the highway for a sign
I head straight for the pink and green neon
Swallow a greasy grilled-cheese sandwich
All the while on the lookout for significance

As we pull out
I twist on the edge of my seat
Hoping for a glimpse of the hospital
With a certain hyphenated name

This is where I was born
I tell the lady who reminds me of my aunts
On her way to Kichatini, Illinois

I was born here
There must be
Something here for me
My mother said
This is where the heat went off and
My arm turned blue
That first winter
After I was born

One Sunday, even Junie Hightower gets saved and joins church. Miss Miriam gets happy and throws her hymn book out of the choir loft. She shouts and cries. She runs down to the altar to kiss her tall boy.

Ruby laughs too loud, drinks too much, pounds you on the back, and throws a softball better than anybody. The mothers suck their teeth and shake their heads. *That Robinson girl walks like a football player.* We know there must be some sin in this, but we can't figure out what it is. When Ruby talks to you, she rubs her jaw. She wraps her arms tight around herself.

IF I WERE AN EPIC POEM

If I were an epic poem
I'd be a fearsome
Warrior or knight
Come from fighting foes
Storming fortresses
Slaying dragons
I'd come bringing
Silver and gold
Scalps and ears
Stories full of
Blood and conquest

Here I am
My steed is a second-hand bike
I come from feeding
Soft poached eggs and soggy toast
To a ninety-four-year-old woman
My tales are her stories of
Babies and husbands dead
Buried long ago
Stories too full of hard work and
Girl I'd start over if I could

If I were a true epic poem
I would be a hero
Tonight I come bringing
Half-bottle brandy libations for
Diana and the Full Moon
Tonight I'm dancing on top of
Your kitchen table
Tonight I am a whispered shouted
Love song
Just the same as you

CABIN FEVER

Three days of snow falling
Word games, knitting and dope
I go up
Into the loft, you come down
I come down, you go up

It's my idea to cut more wood

I kick loose the frozen logs, lug and chuck
You handle the chain saw
As I scramble to keep the cradle full
As I bend and rise and feed the chunks to you
I'm grateful
Grateful for the weight in my arms
Grateful for the rough bark, my gnawed fingers
My clenched back, the cold, sweat
The rip of the saw

You hate the chain saw
You don't understand
Why I need to learn how to use it

How can I say

It is power
A stand-in for touch
I want to use everything
Or get rid of it
I hate words
I want to throw chairs
Break things

How can I explain this to you:

I'll cut wood all night
I won't stop until the stacks
Touch the ceiling
I must
Give you something
That you can use

THE TIRED POEM: LAST LETTER FROM A TYPICAL UNEMPLOYED BLACK PROFESSIONAL WOMAN

So it's a gorgeous afternoon in the park
It's so nice you forget your Attitude
The one your mama taught you
The one that says Don't-Mess-With-Me
You forget until you hear all this
Whistling and lip smacking
You whip around and say
I ain't no damn dog
It's a young guy
His mouth drops open
Excuse me Sister
How you doing
You lie and smile and say
I'm doing good
Everything's cool Brother

Then five minutes later
Hey you Sweet Devil
Hey Girl come here
You tense   sigh   calculate
You know the lean boys and bearded men
Are only cousins and lovers and friends
Sometimes when you say Hey
You get a beautiful surprised smile
Or a good talk

And you've listened to your uncle when he was drunk
Talking about how he has to scuffle to get by and

How he'd wanted to be an engineer
And you talk to Joko who wants to be a singer and
Buy some clothes and get a house for his mother
The Soc. and Psych. books say you're domineering
And you've been to enough
Sisters-Are-Not-Taking-Care-Of-Business discussions
To know where you went wrong
It's decided it had to be the day you decided to go to school
Still you remember the last time you said hey
So you keep on walking
What   you too good to speak
Don't nobody want you no way

You go home   sit on the front steps   listen to
The neighbor boy brag about
How many girls he has pregnant
You ask him if he's going to take care of the babies
And what if he gets taken to court
And what are the girls going to do
He has pictures of them all
This real cute one was supposed to go to college
Dumb broad knew she could get pregnant
I'll just say it's not mine
On the back of this picture of a girl in a cap and gown
It says something like
I love you in my own strange way
Thank you

Then you go in the house
Flip through a magazine and there is
An-Ode-To-My-Black-Queen poem
The kind where the Brother
Thanks all of the Sisters Who Endured
Way back when he didn't have his Shit Together

And you have to wonder where they are now
And you know what happens when you try to resist
All of this Enduring
And you think how this
Thank-you poem is really
No consolation at all
Unless you believe
What the man you met on the train told you
The Black man who worked for the State Department
And had lived in five countries
He said Dear
You were born to suffer
Why don't you give me your address
And I'll come visit

So you try to talk to your friend
About the train and the park and everything
And how it all seems somehow connected
And he says
You're just a Typical Black Professional Woman
Some sisters know how to deal
Right about here
Your end of the conversation phases out
He goes on to say how
Black Professional Women have always had the advantage
You have to stop and think about that one
Maybe you are supposed to be grateful for those sweaty
Beefy-faced white businessmen who try to
Pick you up at lunchtime
And you wonder how many times your friend had
Pennies thrown at him
How many times he's been felt up in the subway
How many times he's been cussed out on the street
You wonder how many times he's been offered
$10 for a piece of himself

$10 for a piece
So you're waiting for the bus
And you look at this young Black man
Asking if you want to make some money
You look at him for a long time
You imagine the little dingy room
It would take twenty minutes or less
You only get $15 for spending all day with thirty kids
Nobody is offering you
Any cash for your poems
You remember again how you have the advantage
How you're not taking care of business
How this man is somebody's kid brother or cousin
And could be your own
So you try to explain how $10 wouldn't pay for
What you'd have to give up
He pushes a handful of sticky crumpled dollars
Into your face and says

Why not
You think I can't pay
Look at that roll
Don't tell me you don't need the money
Cause I know you do
I'll give you fifteen

You maintain your sense of humor
You remember a joke you heard
Well no matter what
A Black Woman never has to starve
Just as long as there are
Dirty toilets and . . .
It isn't funny
Then you wonder if he would at least

Give you the money
And not beat you up
But you're very cool and say
No thanks
You tell him he should spend his time
Looking for someone he cares about
Who cares about him
He waves you off
Get outta my face
I don't have time for that bullshit
You blew it Bitch

Then
(Is it suddenly)
Your voice gets loud
And fills the night street
Your voice gets louder and louder
Your bus comes
The second-shift people file on
The security guards and nurse's aides
Look at you like you're crazy
Get on the damn bus
And remember
You blew it
He turns away
Your bus pulls off
There is no one on the street but you

And then
It is
Very
Quiet

TO BE CONTINUED...

You didn't think I was going to stand
On that corner by myself
My arms and legs like boards
My mouth full of cement
Forever
Now did you
Got myself together
Grabbed the first cab I saw
(Blew my budget for the week)
And got myself home

Lit me some candles and some sandalwood
Put on some Dinah and some Aretha
Took myself a bath
Made myself some grits and eggs
Got on the phone and called up my Gurlfriend

Told her everything
That had had been going down
And you know what she said
She said
Gurl, I know what you mean
I said
For Real
Don't you think I'm crazy

Listen she said
Only crazy you are
Is thinking you owe something to some fool
Come walking up in your face

Intruding on your life
Talking trash

Think about it
How it sound
You feeling ashamed
Cause somebody come treating you
Like you was somebody's pork chop

Don't worry about it Honey
When you got something to say
Say it and don't stop
Just make sure you're talking to somebody
Who shows some interest

Well, I started thinking about my Gurlfriend
And what she said
Then something clicked
Then it dawned on me
Me and my Gurlfriend
You understand
We been friends for years

Now
Whenever I get uptight
I remember what she told me
Keep moving
Keep breathing
Stop apologizing
And keep on talking
When you get scared
Keep talking anyway
Tell the truth like Sojourner Truth

Spill all the beans
Let all the cats out of all the bags

If you are what you eat
You become what you speak
If you free your tongue
Your spirit will follow
Just keep saying it Gurl
You'll get whole
Say it again and again Gurl
You'll get free

If you are what you eat
You become what you speak
Free your tongue and
Your spirit will follow
Free your spirit
No telling what
Could happen

I'VE GOT SOMETHING TO SAY ABOUT THIS: A SURVIVAL INCANTATION FOR BESSIE AND LORRAINE*

I am well aware we are under siege...
But death is not a truth that inspires.

Toni Cade Bambara

I saw it in your eyes
I saw the whole thing played out
I saw myself raped, bludgeoned, bloody
I saw my story reduced to filler on page 49
I said No
No Way

This is it
Think
Remember everything
Now

Later for regrets and why me
Later for guilt and this can't be real

I can see the front-page headlines now
I'm the one on trial
But that's really alright
If only one of us can live through this
I'm the one

I remember everything
In seventh-grade glee club Miz Jay said
Open your mouth wide, girl
You can't look cute and sing
I open my mouth wide
I can't look cute and live

Crazy?
Hell yes I'm crazy
You haven't seen crazy 'til you've seen me
Saving my life

You think I'm stupid
But I'm here thinking
I remember what Big Ed told me
An eyeball is just an eyeball
Eardrums are not made of steel
Anybody's knees give out under
Eight pounds of pressure

Later for the pain
Later for the healing
Later for you, Jack

My mind is made up for me
I am living now
I am sinking my teeth into
Anything I can and I'm
Spitting it back on you
Backonya
Backonya
Backonya

I'm doing what I need to do
Now
I've got something to say about this
I am living
Now

*Bessie is the girlfriend of Bigger Thomas in Richard Wright's *Native Son*. Bigger smashes Bessie's skull as she sleeps and throws her down an airshaft in a desperate attempt to avoid the police. Bessie does not speak during the last moments of her life: "There was a dull gasp of surprise, then a moan." Lorraine is Theresa's lover in Gloria Naylor's *The Women Of Brewster Place*. She is raped by six young men from her neighborhood. Her only words, which she repeats for the rest of her life, are "Please. Please."

IN ANSWER TO THE QUESTION: HAVE YOU EVER CONSIDERED SUICIDE?

Suicide??!!
Gurl, is you crazy?
I'm scared I'm not gonna live long enough
As it is

I'm scared to death of high places
Fast cars
Rare diseases
Muggers
Drugs
Electricity
And folks who work roots

Now what would I look like
Jumping off of something
I got everything to do
And I ain't got time for that
Let me tell you
If you ever hear me
Talking about killing my frail self
Come and get me
Sit with me until that spell passes
Cause it will
And if they ever
Find me laying up somewhere
Don't let them tell you it was suicide
Cause it wasn't

I'm scared of high places
Fast-moving trucks
Muggers
Electricity
Drugs
Folks who work roots
And home-canned string beans

Now with all I got
To worry about
What would I look like
Killing myself

READING LISTS

for Frank D. Rushin

I want
My Dad and I to exchange books to read
I want to give him *Zami* and *The Bluest Eye*
Member Of The Wedding and *The Yearling*

(I want him to ignore The War and the advice
Colored boys need to take up a trade
I want his eyes to be good)

The books I want most to give my father are
The ones I write
The books I want most to read are
The ones he would have written

Union Station Atlanta 1939 Ten Cents A Bag
How I Got Busted Down In This White Man's
Army And Worked My Way Up Again
How I Put It All On The Shelf
And Kept On Doing What I Needed To Do

Horace Chandler wasn't quite right. They say his father hit him. He might be twenty. He might be sixty. He looks like a worried boy. Every day he comes to buy the paper. Every day he stands in the corner by the candy case and stares at the floor. I finally hold out my hand and he puts a dime in it. He glances at me and asks about my aunt and the boys. He touches the brim of his cap as he leaves. One day they say Horace Chandler is dead from malnutrition. They say there was a bag of groceries on the table. Horace Chandler, they say, was never right after what happened with the shovel.

I am afraid of the noise so my Aunt Hilda rides me on the vacuum cleaner. It is silver and blue with metal plates. It's like riding on a spaceship through a galaxy of brown and tan checkerboard tiles. Cousin Dottie and I are watching Dick Clark's "American Bandstand." Dottie is grown. She is dancing. I am sitting on the Electrolux.

THE COWARD

Last night
I stood in the cold dark
With my jeans pulled over my pajamas
And listened to my neighbor
Beat his wife
Only she's not his wife
They just live together

I couldn't move my arms
My breath fluttered in and out
I thought about the police
He would beat her worse after they left
He would come shouting and banging at my door

The police would call it a
Routine Domestic Quarrel
I wasn't so sure I could
Tell the difference
Between the sound of a man
Beating his wife and
The sound of a killing

I held my breath and sneaked to the bathroom
So they wouldn't hear me
As if instead
They'd woken me with their lovemaking

After he was gone
She cried that she didn't understand
I wanted to go to her and hold her
But he slammed in again and it started all over

I guess I'm a coward
If I had been a man I wouldn't've been afraid
I would've beat on the wall
Yelled for them to shut up
So I could get some sleep
I crawled back under the covers
Put the pillow over my head
Went to sleep hoping nothing would happen

This morning his car was gone
I went to her door
I'm sure she's younger than she looks
Her mouth was cut
Her hand was shaking
I couldn't remember
What I wanted to say last night
We're both very reasonable and understanding
In the daylight

I NEVER SEE YOU

But I know you've been here in the night
Every morning
When I walk the dog
I see your ghosts and skeletons
The empty and broken bottles gleaming in the sun

There are new ones every day
No matter how early
Or how late I go
I never see you
But I know you've been here in the night
Sipping, slipping away
By the half pint
Eighty-nine cents worth
At a time

Now
This morning at the bus stop
I look up from my book
And there you are
Standing in the middle of the street
Under the elevated tracks
Leaning on a bright orange girder
With your deep brown face
Turned up toward the grey sky
Water running
From your closed eyes
Into your black beard

Now I see you
And there is nothing I can
Say to you
Nothing I can give

CAMDEN, NEW JERSEY

Two backyards down
Our neighbor is yelling:
Get done, Johnny! Get done!

Johnny is her son.

Then she yells: *Got eight, Wanita!*
Had seven tomatoes,
Now I got eight!

Wanita is her girlfriend

Then it hits me

Our neighbor is a lesbian, a mother,
And just as colored as
Everybody else.

I wonder if I'll be like her

Poking around the garden with my
Afro, jeans, and boy's sneaks
Yelling about tomatoes

Hey, Wanita!
Had seven,
Now I got eight!

THE CONSTRUCTION WORKERS

for Lakey and Leon

I love to see you cutting trim
Hanging doors, tarring roofs

Snapping the chalk line,
Laying bricks with your thick brown hands

You are different from the others
You take nothing for granted

You wear your mud and splatters
Like medals and ribbons

What are you celebrating
What have you won

It's not as simple as it should be
You are working

Working with your mind and
Your own two hands

I see you laying bricks
I see the long years in your eyes

I see you laying bricks
I see you

I see you

UP FROM THE LADDER

Every morning
I am sucked up from my house
Pulled along by the subway
A bundle in a pneumatic tube and
Deposited in this
Concrete tinted-glass
Multi-million dollar mausoleum

It's dark when I leave in the morning
It's dark when I go home

But this building is mine
In a way
I help to make it possible
I fill not one but two
Affirmative Action slots
My folks are proud
And the company gets its
Government Loan
For cheap
(Forty-two grand for the six of us)

My spunky
Cheerful boss
Is very encouraging
Always telling me how bright I am
She marvels at my ability to read and write
On an eighth-grade level
To make simple decisions without her
(Ain't college a-maze-in)
I rewrite convention announcements

For a hardware magazine
While I binge on honey buns and bad coffee

Now don't get me wrong
I'm glad to get this seven thousand before taxes
What with the riot money all dried up
And although I'm underneath The Ladder
I know they need me
I help to keep this whole show
Running

They stand on the sidelines, my uncles, and they watch the young boys running. They see themselves thirty, forty years before. Before the war, before bad knees, big guts and too much Johnny Walker. Otis, they say, remember when you and Georgie Wright were seniors? My Gawd, you were some running fools. Couldn't nothing stop you. They stand on the sidelines in their hats and doubleknits and long coats watching the young boys run. They stand with their hands in their pockets and they laugh and shake their heads. And their eyes shine.

Sundays. After Church. In the summertime. Ride out to The Park and see The Sights. Mint-green double knits. Orange pants. Royal blue mohair. Ummgh. Need to take off all that red. Do rags. Processed heads. Let's get us some Bar-B-Q. Corn-on-the-cob. Best ribs this side of the Mason-Dixie. Let's go have a little taste. Cotton Club. Dreamland. Dew Drop Inn. But watch out for those people from Philly. Always ready to cut somebody. Let's ride out to The Park and see Some Sights. Big yella Caddie. Foxtails on the antenna. G.T.O. Super Sport. Deuce-and-a-Quarter. License plate say: Big Stuff. Four-on-the-floor. Big C. T-Bird. Look at them heads. So many folks in there you can't even see em. Girl, don't let me catch you down that Park. Boy, you better be home before dark. Wear that dress you sweat-back, spike-heel Mama. Shake it but don't break it. Have you ever? I wish he would . . .

A PACIFIST BECOMES MILITANT AND DECLARES WAR

In the old days
I'd see lovers
Strolling and laughing
I'd watch them and smile
And almost let myself wonder
Why I never felt the way they looked

Now I walk down the street with you
And simply because you are always a woman
I get this teetering feeling

Your sudden
Street corner kiss
Accentuates my hesitation
And I realize that in order to care about you
I have to be everything that is in me

Your laughter underscores the
Sick sinking feeling in my stomach and
I know once and for all
If I walk away
Hide from you
I keep on running from myself

Sometimes
When you kiss me on the street
I feel like a sleepwalker
I feel like I just woke up
And I'm standing on a ledge
Twenty-stories high

And I don't know how in the hell I got here
I say to myself
I say Fool
Why don't you go home and act right
You don't have to be here
Pretend it never happened
Pretend you never felt a thing
Except maybe in a nightmare
Or maybe it was a salty, half-shell dream

Go home and act right
But what for
I can never go back
To what never was
I can't force myself into
Somebody else's image

And If I love you
Even just a little bit
I have to love the woman that I am
I have to reach down deep inside
I have to stand and show myself
I have to walk in the world
There is never any going back
Only going forward into the next day
And the day after that

Your full-length street corner kiss
Is seasoned with excitement
And rebellion

O.K.
Then I'm a rebel
I'm a crazy colored woman
Declaring war on my old ways
On all my fear
My choking
My cringing
My hesitation

I break my fast and admit
That I am hungry
I am hungry to care
To become careless
Careful

So I'm a rebel
Get ready for the insurrection
Get ready for the
Rebellion
Uprising
Riot of my kisses

IT WAS IN IBADAN

We were walking in the market
Dizzy from the trays of raw meat
Dutch cloth and bare Black legs
The market women laughed and called to each other
Iyabo   Iyabo
They could see us coming from way down the street
Afros and jeans and shocking light skin
We walked faster and stared at our sneakers in the mud

Later we learned that when a certain
Woman-child is born to a family where the
Mother's mother has died
The women smile and
That child is called Iyabo
She is the spirit of the grandmother come back

So now
When anyone
The Blacks or The Whites
Tells us to be practical
When they speak of politics and
Economics and language barriers
And time and distance and culture
The realities of things
We smile to ourselves
We remember the women in the marketplace
Wrapped in cloth
Babies slung on their backs
Iyabo   Iyabo
They called
She has returned

The old woman with the ramrod back looks me up and down. Humph. . .whose child are you? Look like one of them Williamses. She stands sideways to me on the street corner with her hands behind her back, rocking on her toes. You know I've worked for the Haddons for sixty years, girl. I'm eighty-nine years old and I still work. When I was sick, they brought me my dinner every day for two weeks and I got paid for it. Now what more could I ask for? What more? She stops rocking and looks at me again. Now who's child did you say you was? Ain't you Lizzie's girl?

Other titles from Firebrand Books include:

Artemis In Echo Park, Poetry by Eloise Klein Healy/$8.95

Before Our Eyes, A Novel by Joan Alden/$8.95

Beneath My Heart, Poetry by Janice Gould/$8.95

The Big Mama Stories by Shay Youngblood/$8.95

A Burst Of Light, Essays by Audre Lorde/$9.95

Cecile, Stories by Ruthann Robson/$8.95

Crime Against Nature, Poetry by Minnie Bruce Pratt/$8.95

Diamonds Are A Dyke's Best Friend by Yvonne Zipter/$9.95

Dykes To Watch Out For, Cartoons by Alison Bechdel/$8.95

Dykes To Watch Out For: The Sequel, Cartoons by Alison Bechdel/$9.95

Eight Bullets by Claudia Brenner with Hannah Ashley/$12.95

Exile In The Promised Land, A Memoir by Marcia Freedman/$8.95

Experimental Love, Poetry by Cheryl Clarke/$8.95

Eye Of A Hurricane, Stories by Ruthann Robson/$8.95

The Fires Of Bride, A Novel by Ellen Galford/$8.95

Food & Spirits, Stories by Beth Brant *(Degonwadonti)*/$8.95

Forty-Three Septembers, Essays by Jewelle Gomez/$10.95

Free Ride, A Novel by Marilyn Gayle/$9.95

A Gathering Of Spirit, A Collection by North American Indian Women edited by Beth Brant *(Degonwadonti)*/$10.95

Getting Home Alive by Aurora Levins Morales and Rosario Morales/$9.95

The Gilda Stories, A Novel by Jewelle Gomez/$10.95

Good Enough To Eat, A Novel by Lesléa Newman/$10.95

Humid Pitch, Narrative Poetry by Cheryl Clarke/$8.95

Jewish Women's Call For Peace edited by Rita Falbel, Irena Klepfisz, and Donna Nevel/$4.95

Jonestown & Other Madness, Poetry by Pat Parker/$7.95

Just Say Yes, A Novel by Judith McDaniel/$9.95

The Land Of Look Behind, Prose and Poetry by Michelle Cliff/$8.95

Legal Tender, A Mystery by Marion Foster/$9.95

Lesbian (Out)law, Survival Under the Rule of Law by Ruthann Robson/$9.95

A Letter To Harvey Milk, Short Stories by Lesléa Newman/$9.95

Letting In The Night, A Novel by Joan Lindau/$8.95

Living As A Lesbian, Poetry by Cheryl Clarke/$7.95

Metamorphosis, Reflections on Recovery by Judith McDaniel/$7.95

Mohawk Trail by Beth Brant *(Degonwadonti)*/$7.95

Moll Cutpurse, A Novel by Ellen Galford/$7.95

The Monarchs Are Flying, A Novel by Marion Foster/$8.95

More Dykes To Watch Out For, Cartoons by Alison Bechdel/$9.95

Movement In Black, Poetry by Pat Parker/$8.95

My Mama's Dead Squirrel, Lesbian Essays on Southern Culture by Mab Segrest/ $9.95

New, Improved! Dykes To Watch Out For, Cartoons by Alison Bechdel/$8.95

Normal Sex by Linda Smukler/$8.95

Now Poof She Is Gone, Poetry by Wendy Rose/$8.95

The Other Sappho, A Novel by Ellen Frye/$8.95

Out In The World, International Lesbian Organizing by Shelley Anderson/$4.95

Politics Of The Heart, A Lesbian Parenting Anthology edited by Sandra Pollack
    and Jeanne Vaughn/$12.95

Post-Diagnosis by Sandra Steingraber/$9.95

Presenting...Sister NoBlues by Hattie Gossett/$8.95

Rebellion, Essays 1980–1991 by Minnie Bruce Pratt/$12.95

Restoring The Color Of Roses by Barrie Jean Borich/$9.95

A Restricted Country by Joan Nestle/$9.95

Running Fiercely Toward A High Thin Sound, A Novel by Judith Katz/$9.95

Sacred Space by Geraldine Hatch Hanon/$9.95

Sanctuary, A Journey by Judith McDaniel/$7.95

Sans Souci, And Other Stories by Dionne Brand/$8.95

Scuttlebutt, A Novel by Jana Williams/$8.95

S/he by Minnie Bruce Pratt/$10.95

Shoulders, A Novel by Georgia Cotrell/$9.95

Simple Songs, Stories by Vickie Sears/$8.95

Sister Safety Pin, A Novel by Lorrie Sprecher/$9.95

Skin: Talking About Sex, Class & Literature by Dorothy Allison/$13.95

Spawn Of Dykes To Watch Out For, Cartoons by Alison Bechdel/$9.95

Speaking Dreams, Science Fiction by Severna Park/$9.95

Stardust Bound, A Novel by Karen Cadora/$8.95

Staying The Distance, A Novel by Franci McMahon/$9.95

Stone Butch Blues, A Novel by Leslie Feinberg/$11.95

The Sun Is Not Merciful, Short Stories by Anna Lee Walters/$8.95

Talking Indian, Reflections on Survival and Writing by Anna Lee Walters/$10.95

Tender Warriors, A Novel by Rachel Guido deVries/$8.95

This Is About Incest by Margaret Randall/$8.95

The Threshing Floor, Short Stories by Barbara Burford/$7.95

Trash, Stories by Dorothy Allison/$9.95

We Say We Love Each Other, Poetry by Minnie Bruce Pratt/$8.95

The Women Who Hate Me, Poetry by Dorothy Allison/$8.95

Words To The Wise, A Writer's Guide to Feminist and Lesbian Periodicals &
    Publishers by Andrea Fleck Clardy/$5.95

The Worry Girl, Stories from a Childhood by Andrea Freud Loewenstein/$8.95

Yours In Struggle, Three Feminist Perspectives on Anti-Semitism and
    Racism by Elly Bulkin, Minnie Bruce Pratt, and Barbara Smith/$9.95

**You can buy Firebrand titles at your bookstore, or order them directly
from the publisher (141 The Commons, Ithaca, New York 14850,
607-272-0000).**

**Please include $3.00 shipping for the first book and $.50 for each
additional book.**

A free catalog is available on request.